Price

GW00393885

Lang**Syne**

PUBLISHING

WRITING *to* REMEMBER

LangSyne

PUBLISHING

WRITING *to* REMEMBER

79 Main Street, Newtongrange,
Midlothian EH22 4NA
Tel: 0131 344 0414   Fax: 0845 075 6085
E-mail: info@lang-syne.co.uk
www.langsyneshop.co.uk

Design by Dorothy Meikle
Printed by Printwell Ltd
© Lang Syne Publishers Ltd 2019

ISBN 978-1-85217-667-9

Price

MOTTO:
My help is from the Lord.

CREST:
A lion holding a rose.

NAME variations include:
Pryce

Chapter one:

Origins of Welsh surnames

by Iain Gray

If you don't know where you came from, you won't know where you're going is a frequently quoted observation and one that has a particular resonance today when there has been a marked upsurge in interest in genealogy, with increasing numbers of people curious to trace their family roots.

Main sources for genealogical research include census returns and official records of births, marriages and deaths – and the key to unlocking the detail they contain is obviously a family surname, one that has been 'inherited' and passed from generation to generation.

No matter our station in life, we all have a surname – but it was not until about the middle of the fourteenth century that the practice of being identified by a particular, or 'fixed', surname became commonly established throughout the British Isles.

Previous to this, it was normal for a person to be identified through the use of only a forename.

Wales, however, known in the Welsh language as *Cymru*, is uniquely different – with the use of what are known as patronymic names continuing well into the fifteenth century and, in remote rural areas, up until the early nineteenth century.

Patronymic names are ones where a son takes his father's forename, or Christian name, as his surname.

Examples of patronymic names throughout the British Isles include 'Johnson', indicating 'son of John', while specifically in Scotland 'son of' was denoted by the prefix Mc or Mac – with 'MacDonald', for example, meaning 'son of Donald.'

Early Welsh law, known as *Cyfraith Hywel*, *The Law of Hywel*, introduced by Hywel the Good, who ruled from Prestatyn to Pembroke between 915 AD and 950 AD, stipulated that a person's name should indicate their ancestry – the name in effect being a type of 'family tree.'

This required the prefixes *ap* or *ab* – derived from *mab*, meaning 'son of' being placed before the person's baptismal name.

In the case of females, the suffixes *verch* or *ferch*, sometimes shortened to *vch* or *vz* would be attached to their Christian name to indicate 'daughter of.'

In some cases, rather than being known for

example as *Llewellyn ap Thomas – Llewellyn son of Thomas* – Llewellyn's name would incorporate an 'ancestral tree' going back much earlier than his father.

One source gives the example of *Llewellyn ap Thomas ap Dafydd ap Evan ap Owen ap John* – meaning *Llewellyn son of Thomas son of Dafydd son of Evan son of Owen son of John*.

This leads to great confusion, to say the least, when trying to trace a person's ancestry back to a particular family – with many people having the forenames, for example, of Llewellyn, Thomas, Owen or John.

The first Act of Union between Wales and England that took place in 1536 during the reign of Henry VIII required that all Welsh names be registered in an Anglicised form – with *Hywel*, for example, becoming Howell, or Powell, and *Gruffydd* becoming Griffiths.

An early historical example of this concerns William ap John Thomas, standard bearer to Henry VIII, who became William Jones.

In many cases – as in Davies and Williams – an s was simply added to the original patronymic name, while in other cases the prefix *ap* or *ab* was contracted to *p* or *b* to prefix the name – as in *ab Evan* to form Bevan and *ap Richard* to form Pritchard.

Other original Welsh surnames – such as Morgan, originally *Morcant* – derive from ancient Celtic sources, while others stem from a person's physical characteristics – as in *Gwyn* or *Wynne* a nickname for someone with fair hair, *Gough* or *Gooch* denoting someone with red hair or a ruddy complexion, *Gethin* indicating swarthy or ugly and *Lloyd* someone with brown or grey hair.

With many popular surnames found today in Wales being based on popular Christian names such as John, this means that what is known as the 'stock' or 'pool' of names is comparatively small compared to that of common surnames found in England, Scotland and Ireland.

This explains why, in a typical Welsh village or town with many bearers of a particular name not necessarily being related, they were differentiated by being known, for example, as 'Jones the butcher', 'Jones the teacher' and 'Jones the grocer.'

Another common practice, dating from about the nineteenth century, was to differentiate among families of the same name by prefixing it with the mother's surname or hyphenating the name.

The history of the origins and development of Welsh surnames is inextricably bound up with the nation's frequently turbulent history and its rich culture.

Speaking a Celtic language known as Brythonic, which would gradually evolve into Welsh, the natives were subjected to Roman invasion in 48 AD, and in the following centuries to invasion by the Anglo-Saxons, Vikings and Normans.

Under England's ruthless and ambitious Edward I, the nation was fortified with castles between 1276 and 1295 to keep the 'rebellious' natives in check – but this did not prevent a series of bloody uprisings against English rule that included, most notably, Owain Glyndŵr's rebellion in 1400.

Politically united with England through the first Act of Union in 1536, becoming part of the Kingdom of Great Britain in 1707 and part of the United Kingdom in 1801, it was in 1999 that *Cynulliad Cenedlaethol Cymru*, the National Assembly for Wales, was officially opened by the Queen.

Welsh language and literature has flourished throughout the nation's long history.

In what is known as the Heroic Age, early Welsh poets include the late sixth century Taliesin and Aneirin, author of *Y Gododdin*.

Discovered in a thirteenth century manuscript but thought to date from anywhere between the seventh and eleventh centuries, it refers to the kingdom of Gododdin that took in south-east Scotland and

Northumberland and was part of what was once the Welsh territory known as *Hen Ogledd*, *The Old North*.

Commemorating Gododdin warriors who were killed in battle against the Angles of Bernicia and Deira at Catraith in about 600 AD, the manuscript – known as *Llyfr Aneirin*, *Book of Aneirin* – is now in the precious care of Cardiff City Library.

Other important early works by Welsh poets include the fourteenth century *Red Book of Hergest*, now held in the Bodleian Library, Oxford, and the *White Book of Rhydderch*, kept in the National Library of Wales, Aberystwyth.

William Morgan's translation of the Bible into Welsh in 1588 is hailed as having played an important role in the advancement of the Welsh language, while in 1885 Dan Isaac Davies founded the first Welsh language society.

It was in 1856 that Evan James and his son James James composed the rousing Welsh national anthem *Hen Wlad Fynhadad – Land of My Fathers*, while in the twentieth century the poet Dylan Thomas gained international fame and acclaim with poems such as *Under Milk Wood*.

The nation's proud cultural heritage is also celebrated through *Eisteddfod Genedlaethol Cymru*, the National Eisteddfod of Wales, the annual festival of music, literature and performance that is held across the nation and which traces its roots back to 1176 when Rhys ap Gruffyd, who ruled the territory of Deheubarth from 1155 to 1197, hosted a magnificent festival of poetry and song at his court in Cardigan.

The 2011 census for Wales unfortunately shows that the number of people able to speak the language has declined from 20.8% of the population of just under 3.1 million in 2001 to 19% – but overall the nation's proud culture, reflected in its surnames, still flourishes.

Many Welsh families proudly boast the heraldic device known as a Coat of Arms, as featured on our front cover.

The central motif of the Coat of Arms would originally have been what was borne on the shield of a warrior to distinguish himself from others on the battlefield.

Not featured on the Coat of Arms, but highlighted on page three, is the family motto and related crest – with the latter frequently different from the central motif.

Echoes of a far distant past can still be found in our surnames and they can be borne with pride in commemoration of our forebears.

Chapter two:

Fiery warriors

A name with two different points of origin, 'Price' features prominently in the Welsh historical record.

A patronymic name, it derives from 'ap Rhys', denoting 'son of Rhys' and with 'Rhys 'a Welsh term for 'fiery warrior.'

In this form, the name has been present in Wales from the earliest times, while another source is from the Old French 'pris', meaning 'price' – an occupational surname for someone charged in medieval times with the setting of prices for goods in a local community.

In this form, the name was introduced to British shores in the wake of the Norman Conquest of 1066, a pivotal event in the history of both England and Wales.

It was in 1066 that the death knell of Anglo-Saxon supremacy in England was sounded – with the Anglo-Saxons originally those Germanic tribes who invaded and settled in the south and east of the island of Britain from about the early fifth century.

Composed of the Jutes, from the area of the Jutland Peninsula in modern Denmark, the Saxons from Lower Saxony, in modern Germany and the Angles from the Angeln area of Germany – it was the Angles who gave the name 'Engla land', or 'Aengla land', better known as 'England.'

The Anglo-Saxons held sway in what became England from approximately 550 to 1066, with the main kingdoms those of Sussex, Wessex, Northumbria, Mercia, Kent, East Anglia and Essex – having usurped the power of the indigenous Britons – who referred to them as 'Saeson' or 'Saxones.'

It is from this that the Welsh term for 'English people' of 'Saeson' derives, the Scottish-Gaelic 'Sasannach' and the Irish-Gaelic 'Sasanach'.

We learn from the *Anglo-Saxon Chronicle* how the religion of the early Anglo-Saxons was one that pre-dated the establishment of Christianity in the British Isles.

Known as a form of Germanic paganism, with roots in Old Norse religion, it shared much in common with the Druidic 'nature-worshipping' religion of the indigenous Britons such as the Welsh.

It was in the closing years of the sixth century that Christianity began to take a hold in Britain, while by approximately 690 it had become the 'established' religion of Anglo-Saxon England.

The first serious shock to Anglo-Saxon control came in 789 in the form of sinister black-sailed Viking ships that appeared over the horizon off the island monastery of Lindisfarne, in the northeast of England.

Lindisfarne was sacked in an orgy of violence and plunder, setting the scene for what would be many more terrifying raids on the coastline of not only England, but also of Wales, Ireland and Scotland.

But the Vikings, or 'Northmen', in common with the Anglo-Saxons of earlier times, were raiders who eventually stayed – establishing, for example, trading posts and settlements in Wales at Haverfordwest, Fishguard and Caldey Island.

A further influx of 'Northmen' came with the Conquest – by which time England had become a nation with several powerful competitors to the throne.

In what were extremely complex family, political and military machinations, the monarch was Harold II, who had succeeded to the throne following the death of Edward the Confessor.

But his right to the throne was contested by two powerful competitors – his brother-in-law King Harold Hardrada of Norway, in alliance with Tostig, Harold II's brother, and Duke William II of Normandy.

In what has become known as The Year of Three Battles, Hardrada invaded England and gained victory over the English king on September 20 at the battle of Fulford, in Yorkshire.

Five days later, however, Harold II decisively defeated his brother-in-law and brother at the battle of Stamford Bridge.

But he had little time to celebrate his victory, having to immediately march south from Yorkshire to encounter a mighty invasion force led by Duke William that had landed at Hastings, in East Sussex.

Harold's battle-hardened but exhausted force confronted the Normans on October 14, drawing up a strong defensive position at the top of Senlac Hill and building a shield wall to repel William's cavalry and infantry.

The Normans suffered heavy losses, but through a combination of the deadly skill of their archers and the ferocious determination of their cavalry they eventually won the day.

Morale had collapsed on the battlefield as word spread through the ranks that Harold, the last of the Anglo-Saxon kings, had been killed.

William was declared King of England on December 25, and within an astonishingly short space of time Norman manners, customs and law were imposed on England – a practice destined to be followed in Wales at the point of the sword.

Many Welsh leaders rallied to arms to oppose the Normans – by now more properly known as Anglo-

Normans – and among them was Rhys ap Tewdr, the warrior king of Deheubarth whose popularity among the native Welsh became such that many were given 'Rhys' – from which 'Price' originates – as a forename.

Rhys ap Tewdr boasted an illustrious pedigree, descended as he was through the Dinefur dynasty of the famed Rhodri ap Merfyn, better known to posterity as Rhodri Mawr – Rhodri the Great.

Born in about 820 and succeeding his father when he was aged 24 as King of Gwynedd, he came to control much of what is now modern-day Wales – to the extent that some sources refer to him as 'King of Wales.'

In what were particularly bloody times, he had to contend with both Saxon and Viking invasions – with the Vikings referred to by the Welsh as 'the black gentiles.'

The Welsh historical source known as the *Chronicle of the Princes* records Rhodri killing the Viking leader Gorm in 856 after the Norsemen had ravaged Anglesey.

Confusion surrounds the latter years of Rhodri's kingship, with the chronicle stating that he was killed fighting the Vikings at 'the battle of Sunday' on Anglesey in 873, while other sources assert he was killed four years later along with his brother Gwriad in battle with the Saxons.

His descendant Rhys ap Tewdr, meanwhile, after achieving a series of astounding victories over the Normans that inspired his fellow Welshmen for generations to come, was killed in battle near Brecon in 1093.

Bounded to the west by Cardigan Bay, Merionethshire – known in Welsh as *Meirionnydd or Sir Feirionnyd*, with 'Sir' denoting 'County', and one of the nation's thirteen historic counties, is particularly identified with those who would come to bear the Price name.

One notable family were the Prices of Rhiwlas, in the Merionethshire parish of Llanfor.

One of their early ancestors was Rhys ap Meredydd, also known as Rhys Fawr, who led his men in favour of Henry VII at the 1485 battle of Bosworth, in the modern-day English county of Leicestershire, and which resulted in the death of Henry's rival Richard III.

His son, the ecclesiastic Robert ap Rhys, became one of the king's chaplains, also serving as a chaplain to his successor Henry VIII.

William Price, born at Rhiwlas in 1619, fought as a Royalist colonel during the English Civil War, while his son Roger, born in 1635 and who died in 1719, served for a time as High Sheriff of both Merionethshire and Caernarvon.

Chapter three:

Bards and Druids

Bearers of the proud name of Price have played a major role in both preserving and contributing to the rich and colourful cultural heritage of Wales.

Steeped in the ancient bardic tradition of writing and reciting poetry, the Rev Thomas Price was also a noted antiquarian, historian, essayist, orator, musician, naturalist and educationalist.

Known by his bardic name of *Carnhuanawc*, he was born in 1787 at Pencaerelon, in Llanfihangel-bryn-Pabuan, near Builth Wells, Radnorshire.

Practising as a Church of England curate at Builth Wells, when not diligently ministering to his flock he wrote prolifically in both Welsh and English, and helped Lady Charlotte Guest in her acclaimed translation of the *Mabinogion* – eleven prose stories collected from medieval Welsh manuscripts and which she published between 1838 and 1849.

As an advocate of pan-Celticism, Price not only learned Breton – the language of Brittany – but also encouraged the translation and publication in 1827 of the Breton Bible.

A contributor to a range of not only academic

but also popular journals and recognised as having been a leading figure in the revival of the annual festival of music, literature and performance known as *Eisteddfod Genedlaethol Cymru* – the National Eisteddfod of Wales – he died in 1848.

Described as having been 'one of the most significant figures in nineteenth century Wales and one of the most unusual in Victorian Britain', William Price was born in 1800 at Ty'n-y-coedcae Farm, near Caerphilly, Glamorganshire.

Eccentricity seems to have run in his family – with his father, also named William and a Church of England priest, known for distinctly odd behaviour that included bathing either naked or fully clothed in local ponds and collecting and carrying snakes around in his pockets.

Fluent in Welsh and learning to speak English at school in Machen, his son later qualified as a doctor – becoming a member of the Royal College of Surgeons of England and practicing for a time in London before moving back to his native Wales.

Setting up a medical practice at Craig yr Helfa, in Glyntaff, he remained there for seven years before moving to Pontypridd, Mid Glamorgan, as chief surgeon at a chainworks.

Later appointed medical adviser to the wealthy

Crawshaw family, who owned ironworks in Treforest and Merthyr, he began to immerse himself in Welsh cultural activities such as the Eisteddfod and joining a Neo-Druidic group known as the Society of the Rocking Stone.

These Neo-Druidic groups hearkened back to and attempted to revive what they perceived had been a 'golden age' of the Celtic peoples of Britain, Ireland and Gaul.

Reliable historical sources are frustratingly scant, but the Druids are believed to have formed an educated and highly respected Celtic class.

This exclusive class included bards, law-givers and doctors who practised mysterious ceremonies that involved a cult of the oak tree and mistletoe. They may also have practiced ritual sacrifice, while believing in reincarnation.

It was in the eighteenth century that both England and Wales saw a revival of interest in the Druidic cult, while in the nineteenth century the Welshman Edward Williams – also known as *Iolo Morganwg* – played a significant role in the further development of Neo-Druidism, claiming that he had collected an ancient "Gorsedd of the Bards of the Isles of Britain."

In 1838, William Price attempted to raise sponsorship to build a Druidical museum in Pontypridd, the receipts from which would fund a free school for the poor – but not enough sponsors were forthcoming.

Price's reaction was to pen an angry letter to his local newspaper, stating that people were "ignoring their immortal progenitors, to whom you owe your very existence as a civilised people."

A leading light of his local Chartist movement – with Chartists being those who sought the franchise for all men regardless of wealth or rank – Price had to flee into exile in France as a political dissident in 1839 after supplying fellow Chartists with weapons in a bid to foment revolution.

It was while visiting the Louvre, in Paris, that he chanced upon a stone bearing a mysterious inscription which, he claimed, was an ancient prophecy stating that "a man would come in the future to reveal the true secrets of the Welsh language and to liberate the Welsh people."

Returning to Wales and immersing himself even deeper in the Druidic mysteries, he entered into what was perceived at the time as a 'scandalous' unmarried relationship with a local woman, Ann Morgan, declaring that marriage was wrong because it enslaved women.

Ann bore him a daughter in 1842 and Price 'baptised' her at the Rocking Stone at Pontypridd, naming her *Gwenholian Ialles Morganwg* – Welsh for Gwenhiolan, Countess of Glamorgan.

By now habitually dressed in emerald green clothing and a fox fur head dress and calling himself 'Lord of the Southern Welsh', he was forced to flee again to France, in 1861, after incurring hefty debts.

Returning five years later, and with Ann Morgan now dead and his daughter having left to lead her own life, he set up a medical practice in Llantrisant, Mid Glamorgan.

Taking a young farmer's daughter, Gwenllian Llewelyn, as his new partner, the couple had a son – whom he named *Iesu Grist*, Welsh for Jesus Christ – but the child died only five months later.

Believing that it was an offence against nature to bury a corpse because it polluted the earth, Price was arrested by the police in January of 1884 after attempting to cremate his son on the summit of a hill on the outskirts of Llantrisant.

In a sensational trial in Cardiff, charged with attempting to perform a cremation, Price argued that while the law did not state cremation was legal, it also did not state that it was illegal.

In a landmark ruling, the judge agreed – paving the way for the first official cremation, at Woking, in 1885, followed by the Cremation Act of 1902.

Price died in 1893 and, before a crowd of up to 20,000, he was cremated on the summit of the same hill where, after the judge's ruling, he had finally been allowed to cremate his son.

Depicted dressed in his fox skin head dress and with his arms outstretched, a statue to the colourfully eccentric William Price was unveiled in Llantrisant in 1982, while a memorial garden was named for him ten years later.

Chapter four:

On the world stage

A master of the horror genre of films, Vincent Leonard Price Jr., better known as Vincent Price, was born in 1911 in St Louis, Missouri.

From a wealthy background, his grandfather Vincent Clarence Price was the inventor of the first cream of tartar baking powder – Dr Price's Baking Powder – while his father was president of the National Candy Company.

Graduating from Yale University when he was aged 22 with a degree in art history, the future actor then studied for a degree in fine arts at the University of London – but the lure of the stage proved too strong.

By 1936 he was appearing in an American production of the stage play *Victoria Regina* and, two years later, made his screen debut in *Service de Luxe*.

Other early screen credits include the 1940 *Brigham Young* and, from 1944, *The Keys of the Kingdom* – having already ventured into the horror genre with the 1939 *Tower of London*.

While establishing himself as an accomplished actor not only in the chilling realm of horror with films that include *The Ten Commandments*, he became best known for a series of horror films that include the 1960 *The House of Usher*, the 1961 *The Pit and the Pendulum* and, from 1964, *The Masque of the Red Death*.

Film credits in the 1970s include *Theatre of Blood*, while his distinctive voice was also in high demand outside the film world – providing a voiceover, for example, for rock star Alice Cooper's 1975 solo album *Welcome to My Nightmare* and for Michael Jackson's 1982 album *Thriller*.

An inductee of the St Louis Walk of Fame, his last major film role – three years before his death in 1993 – was that of the inventor in *Edward Scissorhands*.

From the big screen to the small screen, **Tom Price** is the Welsh actor born in Monmouth in 1980.

Television credits include the Channel 5 comedy sketch show *Swinging*, the Doctor Who spin-off *Torchwood* and, from 2010, *Secret Diary of a Call Girl*, while he is also the creator of the Channel 4 quiz show *Wogan's Perfect Recall*.

A granddaughter of the late English cricketer John Price, who played for Worcestershire, **Claire Price** is the actress best known for her role, starring beside Ken Stott, of Detective Sergeant Siobhan Clarke in the television crime drama *Rebus*.

Other television credits include *Dalziel and*

Pascoe, *Agatha Christie's Poirot* and *Murder in Mind*, while as a stage actress her role in *The Pride* won her the award for Best Supporting Performance at the 2011 UK Theatre Awards.

On the big screen, her role as Alice in *Jump* won her Best Actress Award at the 2012 British Film Festival.

Of German, Irish and Korean descent, **Lindsay Jayln Price** is the American actress known for her television roles in *Lipstick Jungle* and *Beverley Hills, 90210*.

Born in 1976 in Arcadia, California, other television credits include the soaps *The Bold and the Beautiful* and *All My Children*.

With the popular Price spelling variation of 'Pryce', **Jonathan Pryce** is the Welsh actor born in 1947 in Carmel, Flintshire.

The recipient of a CBE and a Fellow of the Royal Welsh College of Music and Drama, his many film credits include the 1996 *Evita*, the 1997 James Bond film *Tomorrow Never Dies* and, from 2002, *Pirates of the Caribbean: Curse of the Black Pearl*.

Also an acclaimed stage actor, he is the recipient of two Tony Awards – for his performances in the 1977 Broadway production of *Comedians* and the 1991 *Miss Saigon*.

Voted the Royal Television Society's Young Journalist of the Year in 2000, **Matthew Price** was born in London in 1972.

Beginning his journalistic career as a trainee local radio reporter and then reporting for the BBC children's television news programme *Newsround*, he has since acted as the BBC's Belgrade correspondent, covered the Iraq War, been based in Jerusalem as a Middle East correspondent and in Brussels as BBC's Europe Correspondent.

Nominated in 2010 along with producer Ian Sherwood and cameraman Chuck Tayman for an Emmy Award for their coverage of Mexico's drugs wars, he was named News Journalist of the Year at the 2011 Sony Radio Awards for his coverage of the Haitian earthquake.

Behind the camera lens, **Richard Price**, born in 1949 in The Bronx, New York City is the American novelist and screenwriter whose first novel *The Wanderers* was adapted for a film of the name in 1992 as was his novel *Clockers*.

As a screenwriter, his credits include the 1986 *The Color of Money*, the 1993 *Mad Dog and Glory* and the 2000 version of *Shaft*, while he also wrote scripts for the television police drama series *The Wire*.

Also the author of the 2008 novel *Lush Life*, he

is a recipient of an American Academy of Arts and Letters Award in Literature.

Born in 1941, **Roger Price** is the English television producer who created the children's science fiction series *The Tomorrow People* in addition to *Junior Points of View*, *You Must Be Joking* and *Pauline's Quirkes*.

From the screen to the world of music, **Alan Price** born in 1942 in Fatfield, Co. Durham is the English musician who in 1962 was a founding member of the Tyneside band The Animals.

Originally known as the Alan Price Rhythm and Blues Combo and with Price on keyboards, he left the band in 1965 to form the Alan Price Set, enjoying a number of hits that include *Hi-Lili, Hi-Lo*, the 1967 Randy Newman song *Simon Smith and His Amazing Dancing Bear*, *The House That Jack Built* and *Don't Stop the Carnival*.

Along with Georgie Fame, he also had chart success with the 1971 *Rosetta*, while the pair also featured regularly on the *Morecambe and Wise* television show.

Also a writer of acclaimed scores for films that include the 1973 *O Lucky Man!* and the 1987 *The Whales of August*, he composed and sang *Time and Tide* – the theme tune for the 1982 film *The Plague Dogs* –

and also composed the score for the musical *Andy Capp*.

On American shores, **Lloyd Price**, also known as "Mr Personality", from his hit song *Personality*, is the rhythm and blues vocalist best known for his 1952 *Lawdy Miss Clawdy*.

Born in 1933 in Kenner, Louisiana, and with other hits that include *I'm Gonna Get Married* and *Stagger Lee*, he is an inductee of the Louisiana Music Hall of Fame – while his home town annually celebrates "Lloyd Price Day."

A bass guitarist with British bands that have included The Move, Sight and Sound, Light Fantastic and Wizzard, Richard Price, better known as **Rick Price**, was born in Birmingham in 1944.

With The Move from 1969 to 1970, he later played with former band colleague Carl Wayne in Light Fantastic, while with another former bandmate, Ron Wood, he played in Wizzard and had hits with the band that include *See My Baby Jive* and the Christmas pop classic *I Wish It Could Be Christmas Everyday*.

Also having had a songwriting partnership with Mike Sheridan, with whom he collaborated on the 1970 album *This Is to Certify: Gemini Anthology*, he is married to Dianne Lee of the 1970s' duo Peters and Lee.

In a much different musical genre, Margaret

Bernice Price was the internationally acclaimed Welsh soprano more formally known as **Dame Margaret Bernice Price**.

Born in 1951 near Caerphilly, South Wales, and overcoming the physical handicap of being born with deformed legs and having to undergo surgery that left her in pain for the rest of her life, she was aged 15 when she won a scholarship to Trinity College of Music, London.

Training as a mezzo soprano, she later joined the Ambrosian Singers and performed with them on the soundtrack for the 1961 film *El Cid*, starring Charlton Heston.

Her operatic debut came a year later as Cherubino in a production at the Welsh National Theatre of Mozart's *The Marriage of Figaro*, while she reprised the role a year after this at the Royal Opera House, Covent Garden.

Performing later with Cologne Opera, Bavarian State Opera and, in 1985, with the Metropolitan Opera, New York, she was famed for her Mozart portrayals – including Pamina in *The Magic Flute*.

Also famed for her recording of Wagner's *Tristan and Isolde*, she died in 2011, eight years after being made a Dame Commander of the Order of the British Empire (DBE) for her services to music.

Bearers of the Price name have also excelled in the highly competitive world of sport.

Born in 1945 in Hendy, Carmarthenshire, Terence Graham Price, better known as **Terry Price**, was not only a Welsh dual-code international rugby union and rugby league player, but also a player in American football.

Playing at club level in rugby union as a fullback for Llanelli and, in rugby league, for Bradford Northern, he also played for the British Lions and Great Britain.

Tried out as a placekicker for the American football team the Buffalo Bills in 1971, he died in a road accident in 1993 while helping a motorist whose car had broken down.

On the golf course, **Richard N. Price III** is the American golfer who plays on the Nationwide Tour.

Born in 1968 in Reading, Pennsylvania, he was the winner of the Xerox Classic in 2005 and, three years later, the Nationwide Tour Players Cup.

In the creative world of the written word, **Anthony Price** is the award-winning English author of espionage thrillers born in 1928 in Hertfordshire.

Known for his *Dr David Audley/Colonel Jack Butler* series of novels, his many awards include a Gold Dagger Award for his 1974 *Other Paths to Glory*, while

Chessgame was adapted in 1983 for a six-part television series.

A vice-president of the Romantic Novelists' Association, **Evadne Price**, born Eva Grace Price in 1888 in Merewether, New South Wales, and who also wrote under the pseudonym of Helen Zenna Smith, was the Australian-British writer who, in addition to her romantic novels, also created the popular children's books character Jane Turpin.

Also noted for her semi-autobiographical novel *Not So Quiet: Stepdaughters of War*, she died in 1985, aged 97.

In the world of contemporary tabloid newspaper and reality television celebrity, **Katie Price** was born in 1978 in Brighton, East Sussex.

Taking the Price surname when she was aged ten from her stepfather, it was as a glamour model for a tabloid newspaper that, using the pseudonym Jordan, she first achieved fame.

This led to modelling work for a range of magazines, while television work has included the reality television show *I'm a Celebrity … Get Me Out of Here!*

It was in the 2004 series of this show that she met and later married the pop star Peter Andre, but the couple later divorced.

Also married for a time to the professional 'cage fighter' Alex Reid and, from 2013, to the builder and part-time stripper Kieran Hayler, she has also dated a number of sports stars and other celebrities who include the footballer Dwight Yorke – the father of one of her five children.

A successful businesswoman, with her own ranges of perfume and lingerie, her books of autobiography and novels – ghost-written by Rebecca Farnworth – have been best-sellers.